IMAGES
*of America*

# ZIPPO

## MANUFACTURING COMPANY

IMAGES
*of America*

# ZIPPO
## MANUFACTURING COMPANY

Linda L. Meabon
Foreword by George B. Duke

ARCADIA
PUBLISHING

Published by Arcadia Publishing
Charleston, South Carolina

Library of Congress Catalog Card Number: 2003106546

For all general information, contact Arcadia Publishing:
Telephone 843-853-2070
Fax 843-853-0044
E-mail sales@arcadiapublishing.com
For customer service and orders:
Toll-free 1-888-313-2665

Visit us on the Internet at www.arcadiapublishing.com.

# CONTENTS

# ACKNOWLEDGMENTS

A special thank-you to Debbie Curtin and Steve Mahon at Zippo Manufacturing Company for their assistance with photographs and layout. A thank-you goes to Pat Grandy and members of the marketing team for their editing assistance. Also, thanks to Tom Hendryx for supplying photographs of the Zippo Ski Slope and the Zippo Riders and to Wendell Crawford for supplying detailed historical information about the Zippo Riders.

# FOREWORD

"Build your product with integrity, stand behind it 100 percent, and success will follow." This well-renowned quote by my grandfather George G. Blaisdell was truly the cornerstone upon which he created his beloved Zippo lighter and the company that stands behind it—the Zippo Manufacturing Company of Bradford, Pennsylvania. As we celebrate in 2003 the 400-millionth lighter manufactured by the company, I truly believe that my grandfather had the vision and belief to foresee the huge success we enjoy today. Zippo lighters are sold on nearly every continent and throughout more than 120 countries.

From the very beginning, my grandfather realized Zippo's most valuable resource was its employees and the community of Bradford. Without the hard work and dedication of the employees, as well as the support of the community, Zippo, no doubt, would have been just another company that would have come and gone.

The Zippo lighter has a range of appeal to its owners. The fact that the company placed date codes on the bottom of the lighters have made Zippo lighters very collectible. Actually, this was done so that the company could track the types of repairs that were performed. Little did Grandpa know that these date codes would make these lighters so collectable.

Zippo lighters are very simplistic in design and a very dependable source of flame. The design of the lighter has been virtually the same for more than 70 years. Zippo's famous lifetime guarantee that "it works, or we fix it free" ensures that a Zippo owner will have a functional Zippo lighter forever. Certainly this world-famous guarantee has helped to build the immense integrity that the brand enjoys today.

The Zippo lighter, having been through many wars, including World War II, the Korean War, the Vietnam War, and more recent conflicts, is a piece of history.

One of appealing attributes about Zippo lighters is the wide range of styles and decorations that have been have been available over the years. One can choose the ideal lighter to reflect one's personality. These decorations include metal engravings, emblems, corporate logos, full-colored images, and a large range of different finishes.

Displayed in this book are rarely seen photographs from our archives, which we are pleased to share with the general public. We hope to enlighten Zippo enthusiasts and history buffs alike.

In 1997, the Zippo/Case Visitors Center was opened to display our beautiful historical lighters and the chronological history of the company. People come to Bradford from all over the world to visit the birthplace of the Zippo lighter. The fact that Zippo lighters are manufactured here helps to put Bradford on the world map.

In the past several years, I have traveled extensively throughout the world, and it always amazes me to see the popularity and interest in the Zippo lighter. I have been told that people look at Zippo as almost a way to live one's life—with simplicity, yet deep-rooted integrity. These are values that people love to aspire to and embrace in their lives.

Early in my life, I knew that I wanted to work for my grandfather at Zippo. I wrote to him shortly after I graduated from college to ask for the opportunity. The past 26 years have been remarkable for me, as I have seen the company grow and prosper in many different ways. In keeping with my grandfather's basic business philosophies, Zippo is the most popular and most successful lighter company in the world. As I look towards the future, I have every belief that Zippo will remain a family-owned-and-operated business through my two sons, George Jr. and Grant.

I would like to acknowledge and thank my mother, Sarah B. Dorn, for her dedication to her father's company and her support of me in my career at Zippo. Without this support, Zippo would not be where it is today. Her role in this company has certainly been an extension of her father's values and her undying love for Zippo.

I would also like to recognize Linda Meabon, our historian and archivist, for the extensive work and dedication she has put forth in helping to make this book a reality.

In closing, I believe that our founder, George G. Blaisdell, my grandfather, would be extremely proud and delighted to see the remarkable worldwide success of his beloved company, which was started in a room above the Rickerson and Pryde Garage, here in Bradford in 1932.

—George B. Duke, Chairman of the Board

# One

# THE BEGINNING

The first Zippo factory was located on the second floor of the Rickerson and Pryde building. George G. Blaisdell paid $10 a month rent for the room over an automobile garage. Here, the text in the large window reads, " 'Zippo' Windproof Lighter." A portion of this building still stands today at the wye intersection of Pine and East Washington Streets in Bradford.

George Blaisdell is shown in the foreground as a young boy growing up in Bradford. George Grant Blaisdell was born June 5, 1895, to Philo and Sarah Blaisdell in Bradford. The family home still stands at the corner of Congress Street and Blaisdell Avenue.

George Blaisdell (fifth from the left) is seen here with a group of friends outside of the Bradford Billiard Parlor.

An Austrian lighter inspired George Blaisdell to invent the Zippo lighter. Smoking on the porch of the Bradford Country Club, George Blaisdell asked local businessman Dick Dresser why he was all dressed up and using such an awkward lighter. Dresser replied, "Well, it works." That statement stuck with George Blaisdell, and he set out to produce a lighter that required one-handed operation, was windproof, and was guaranteed to work.

Shown here is the inside of the first Zippo factory in the Rickerson and Pryde building. The first factory had three employees, including George Blaisdell, who also managed sales of the lighter. The 1930s were not the ideal time to start a business because of the lingering effects of the Depression.

The attached tag on the prototype of the first Zippo lighter reads, "First Zippo lighter, Do not touch." The note is in George Blaisdell's handwriting. Now a museum exhibit in the Zippo/Case Visitors Center, this lighter was found tucked away in George Blaisdell's desk after he passed on. In 2000, the History Channel filmed this lighter and portrayed the story of its discovery in a segment of *History's Lost and Found*.

Produced in 1933, the first Zippo lighters were rectangular in shape, and a 1/4-inch taller than Zippo lighters produced today, with the entire hinge soldered to the outside of the lighter case. The case and inside lighting mechanism were cut from brass tubing. Small rectangular brass pieces were soldered into the top and bottom to complete the lighter case. Later in 1933, decorative lines were added to make the lighter more attractive. The first patent for the Zippo lighter, patent No. 2032695, was issued March 3, 1936.

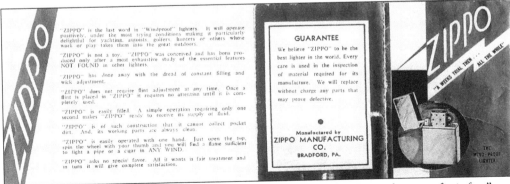

The first printed Zippo guarantee is seen here. The guarantee that "it works or we fix it free" was placed in the gift box of every Zippo lighter. Even today, if your Zippo lighter or any other genuine Zippo product fails to work, it will be repaired at no charge when returned to the Zippo factory. The Zippo guarantee's word-of-mouth advertising was the first advertising for Zippo lighters.

George Blaisdell proudly displays a giant replica of his Zippo lighter in his office at 36 Barbour Street *c*. the late 1940s.

# Two

# THE EARLY YEARS

The Zippo factory on Barbour Street can be seen to the left of the houses in this March 1953 photograph.

This building at 36 Barbour Street was the first Zippo real-estate purchase. The factory was located in the back of the building, and the office was in the front. This building is now used for storage and is located next to the armory. This is how the building appeared in the 1940s.

Zippo acquired several buildings on Barbour Street in the late 1940s, enabling the factory to be located across the street from the office building. The sign above the door in this picture reads "Zippo Factory Offices."

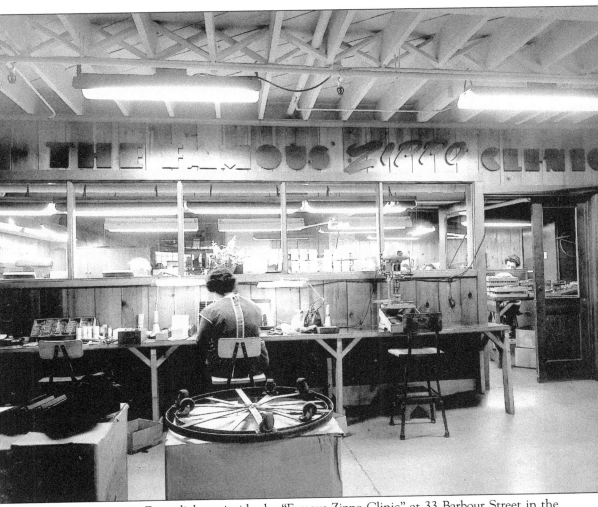

Employees repair Zippo lighters inside the "Famous Zippo Clinic" at 33 Barbour Street in the late 1940s. The repair clinic was George Blaisdell's favorite department. He visited it daily, seeking customer feedback and information. He used Zippo consumer information to make slight improvements to the Zippo lighter and for ideas for new designs to be imprinted on the lighters.

NOV 2 1 1939
_____19____

We received your lighter which is going forth, by parcel post to you today, at no charge.

We thank you for the opportunity of servicing your lighter and,—don't forget, no one has ever been charged for the repair of a ZIPPO LIGHTER.

Yours truly,

ZIPPO MANUFACTURING COMPANY.

This postcard, dated November 21, 1939, was used in the Zippo Repair Clinic. A postcard was sent to each customer advising that his or her Zippo lighter had been repaired and was being returned to him or her by parcel post the same day.

Zippo repair technicians restore Zippo lighters to first-class mechanical condition, then return them to their owners at no charge for many more years of useful service.

Dale Hutton is seen here outside of the Zippo office building at 36 Barbour Street in 1943. A lifelong Zippo employee, Dale later became foreman of the engraving department. He was a master at his craft and could always find a way to engrave the most difficult designs on the Zippo lighter.

Zippo office secretaries Ruth Brocklehurst (left) and Ann Conley are taking a break near the Zippo facility at 36 Barbour Street in 1942.

Zippo employees traveled by train to the 1949 Ice Follies in Buffalo, New York. Each year, George Blaisdell reserved a sizeable block of seats and invited his Zippo employees to be his guests at the Sunday afternoon performance of the Ice Follies. George Blaisdell appreciated his employees and the people of Bradford. He often stated, "If it weren't for the people of Bradford, there would be no Zippo; Zippo will always support Bradford and the surrounding area residents."

Jay Rizzuti, a Bradford resident, takes a jump on the Zippo Ski Slope, located at the far end of Callahan City Park off Interstate Parkway, in 1947. George Blaisdell subsidized the ski slope and all related maintenance, including the automatic rope tow. His only request was that all residents of Bradford and the area would be permitted to use the slope.

The Zippo Ski Slope was the scene of many ski meets and competitions. This competition took place on February 23, 1947. Many of the photographs of the ski slope that appear in this book are courtesy of Tom Hendryx, who skied the slope daily with friends during the winter.

This group was part of the Zippo Motorcycle Riders club. Harley motorcycle riders in the area organized the club in the early 1950s. Pictured from left to right are Howard Eschrich, Cecil Smith, Fred Crawford, Virginia Crawford, and Gloria Price. (Courtesy of Tom Hendryx.)

## ZIPPO MOTORCYCLE RIDERS

### MEMBERSHIP CARD

Name __Cecil Smith__

Address _____

City and State __Custer City, Pa.__

*J. Maynard Price - Pres.*　　　No. ____

Cecil Smith's official Zippo Motorcycle Riders membership card was signed by club president J. Maynard Price. (Courtesy of Tom Hendryx.)

Cecil Smith (left) and Maynard Price are pictured here with their torn-down Harley motorcycle engine. These fellows were always tinkering, trying to get their motorcycles to go faster. (Courtesy of Tom Hendryx.)

Waverly Hull poses in her official Zippo Riders shirt. Waverly and her husband were members of the Zippo Motorcycle Riders. G.O. Heinzman, local Harley Davidson dealer and school chum of George Blaisdell, told Blaisdell about the local motorcycle club and their need for sponsorship. George Blaisdell responded by purchasing special club shirts for the members. The group made Blaisdell an honorary club member and named the organization the Zippo Motorcycle Riders. Blaisdell continued his support of the Zippo Riders, sponsoring sanctioned Harley Davidson rides. (Information courtesy of Wendell Crawford.)

23

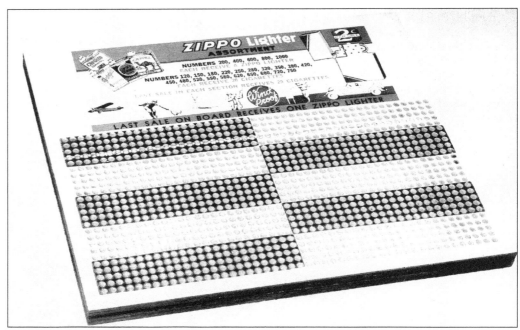

Punchboards were the first official form of advertising for Zippo lighters. Punchboards were used from the mid-1930s, and in 1937, 65,000 Zippo lighters were sold on punchboards. Considered a game of chance, punchboards were outlawed in 1940.

Zippo's first national advertisement ran in the December 1937 edition of *Esquire* magazine. George Blaisdell borrowed $750 from the local bank to place the advertisement. Unfortunately, the advertisement did not produce the expected results because Zippo did not have an adequate distribution network in place. Windy represented the windproof feature of the Zippo lighter in many Zippo advertisements in the 1930s and 1940s.

A 500-piece order from Kendall in 1935 marked the beginning of the Zippo specialty advertising business. The 1937 advertisement shows Zippo lighters imprinted with "metallique" logos and initials. Metalliques were small pieces of metal lace that were glued onto the lighter. The background of the metallique was hand painted using enamel paint.

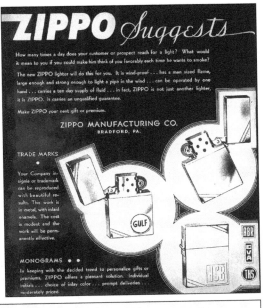

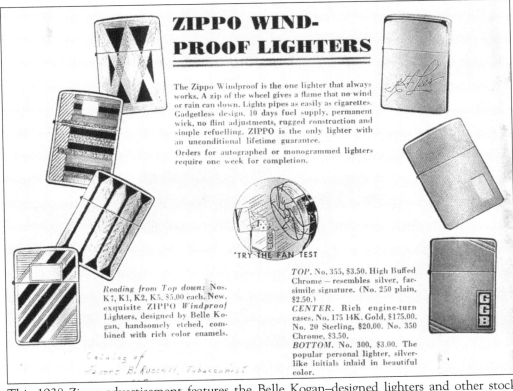

This 1938 Zippo advertisement features the Belle Kogan–designed lighters and other stock lighters that could be personalized using metallique initials or stock metallique designs for the cost of $1. Kogan was a well-known New York designer who emigrated from Russia. Numerous early advertisements encouraged consumers to "try the fan test" to prove the windproof design of the Zippo lighter.

The neon sign on top of the Zippo Canada plant was similar to the neon sign on top of the Barbour Street office building in Bradford. The Canadian sign was dismantled in 2002, however, the neon sign in Bradford is still visible from Main Street.

The office and factory of the Zippo Manufacturing Company Canada are located in Niagara Falls, Ontario. Zippo Canada was established in 1949 to improve distribution outside of the United States. Zippo Canada closed its doors on July 31, 2002.

Wyona Pederson Hyde checks orders received at the Zippo Canada office. Wyona later became general manager of Zippo Canada.

Employees engrave lighters at the Zippo Canada factory. All Zippo lighters were produced in the Bradford manufacturing plant. Lighters for Zippo Canada had the bottom of the case and the inside lighting mechanism stamped "Niagara Falls, Ontario." Zippo lighters bearing a Niagara Falls bottom stamp were assembled, engraved, packaged, and shipped from the Canadian facility. Zippo Canada, in operation from 1949 to 2002, was the only Zippo Manufacturing Company facility outside of Bradford.

# ZIPPO'S $300,000 Wheel at work!

A problem with the flint was discovered in 1946. George Blaisdell stopped all shipping of lighters and hired renowned metallurgists at the cost of $300,000 to perfect the flint wheel of the lighter. Amazingly, all Zippo employees were kept on the payroll until the problem was solved and production of the lighter resumed.

Inspired by the 1918 Pep-O-Mint Lifesaver truck, George Blaisdell purchased a new 1947 Chrysler Saratoga at a cost of $2,048 from Bauschards, a local Chrysler dealership, and sent the car to Gardner Displays in Pittsburgh for customization. When finished, the car had giant chrome lighter doors with lids that opened and closed, a grill with the word "Zippo," lettering on its doors plated in 24-karat gold, and removable neon flames that embellished the giant lighters. The Zippo car led numerous parades within the 48 states and was driven by Dick O'Day, a Bradford salesman.

Zippo lighters engraved with the original Zippo car design were given out wherever the car made an appearance. The Zippo car was not without problems. The weight of the giant lighters caused the tires of the car to blow out, and the armor-plated fenders made it impossible to jack the car up to change the tires. The car was sent to Toohey Motors in Pittsburgh for a heavier chassis design to support the weight of the giant doors. The renovation proved to be very costly and enthusiasm for the renovation waned. In later years, Zippo attempted to locate the Zippo car but found that Toohey Motors was no longer in business, and the Zippo car had disappeared, never to be seen again.

George Blaisdell sports one of his trademark flashy bow ties.

# Three

# ZIPPO GOES TO WAR

Bradford resident Frank Kemick served as a medic with the 112th Armored Division in World War II. Proud of his Bradford roots, Kemick painted the Zippo lighter and the words "Bradford, Pa. Home of the Zippo" on the doors of his ambulance. (Courtesy of F.J. "Skip" Kemick.)

World War II correspondent Ernie Pyle wrote about the Zippo lighter in his articles from the front lines, calling it "the most coveted item on the battlefield." George Blaisdell sent Pyle 50 to 100 Zippo lighters each month to distribute by lottery among the GIs. As a result, the Zippo lighter gained worldwide recognition during World War II.

The World War II Black Crackle Zippo lighter, made from steel due to the lack of brass, was painted with thick black crackle paint and baked, producing a slightly rough surface. The distinctive "click" of the black crackle lighter when opened and closed served as a signal between troops. The lighter was also used to heat food (sometimes in a helmet), to light fires, and for hammering.

The shortest war story ever written was recorded on a Zippo lighter. Ernie Pyle was on board the USS *Cabot* in March 1945. The troops did not know where they were headed, but rumor had it something big was coming. A young officer was prodding Pyle to tell where they were headed. Pyle would not say but asked the young officer for his lighter. Pyle scratched something on the bottom of the lighter and handed it back saying, "Put the lighter in your pocket and don't look at it until the orders are opened." The call to orders was given, and the young officer took the Zippo lighter from his pocket. "Tokyo" was scratched on the bottom.

ZIPPO...THE LIGHTER THAT WORKS.

The owner of this black crackle lighter sent it to Zippo for repair explaining that he carried the lighter in his pocket during the first Philippine sea battle. The owner sent specific instructions with the lighter: "Please don't refinish it. That would spoil its personality." Zippo did not refinish it but did fix it for free and returned it to the owner in first-class working order.

**"He Gets to Sleep By Counting ZIPPO Lighters"**

Those of us back home will have to continue to "dream" about that genuine ZIPPO *Windproof* LIGHTER that always works at the zip of the wheel. No consumer sales until the boys on the high seas and the fighting fronts are fully supplied.

WARNING: Watch out for imitations claimed to be ZIPPO, or "ZIPPO type"—you may pay a high black-market price for something that won't work—so wait a little longer for a real ZIPPO Lighter.

*Most dealers carry genuine ZIPPO Flints and Fluid.*

ZIPPO MFG. CO.
Dept. C,
Bradford, Pa.

*No one ever paid a cent to repair a ZIPPO*

 I'VE GONE TO WAR SO BUY WAR STAMPS INSTEAD

**ZIPPO** *Windproof* **LIGHTER**

This World War II Zippo advertisement stated that all Zippo lighters produced were being sent to the military and could not be purchased stateside. The small lighter figure at the lower right reinforced this with the caption, "I've gone to war so buy war stamps instead." The advertisement further warns consumers about imitation Zippo or Zippo–type lighters that may be marketed as genuine Zippo lighters.

The Zippo lighters produced during the Korean War were made from steel, then chrome plated. As a tribute to the Korean War veterans, Zippo produced a limited edition, two-piece brass lighter set in 1996.

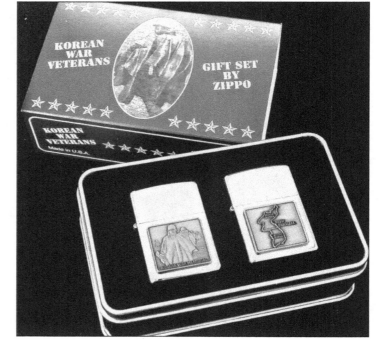

Thousands of Zippo lighters were carried by troops from all branches of the military during the Vietnam War. Many lighters were customized in small Vietnamese shops or by the soldiers themselves with sentiments relating to the war.

This World War II advertisement publicizes the personal attachment of a military man to his Zippo lighter.

A sand-camouflage, matte-finish Desert Storm lighter was produced for the 1991 Gulf War.

These 2003 Zippo lighters showed support for the military troops of Operation Iraqi Freedom.

# *Four*

# THE GROWTH YEARS

This is a classic George G. Blaisdell photograph—the founder and his lighter.

The Zippo truck is locked and loaded at the Barbour Street plant in this early 1960s photograph.

Huge fuel storage tanks are buried in front of 36 Barbour Street in preparation for the new Zippo Lighter Fuel Company.

The opening of the new office building provided the opportunity for Zippo Lighter Fuel to locate in the former office and factory at 36 Barbour Street.

The first Zippo manufacturing facility located on Congress Street in Bradford is shown here in 1953. Zippo purchased three acres of ground and erected a cement-block building to house the case fabrication and chrome plating operations. Prior to the addition of this facility, case fabrication and chrome plating had been subcontracted to Bush Brothers of Olean, New York, and Backus Novelty Company of Smethport, Pennsylvania. This property was part of the old racetrack in Bradford.

The "Home of the Windproof Lighter" Zippo logo sign is being erected at the Congress Street facility in the early 1960s.

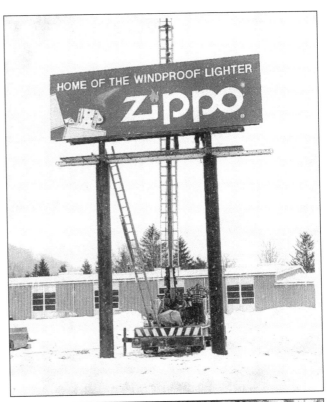

An aerial photograph of the Zippo Congress Street facility in the mid-1960s shows the fabrication and plating operations building (left, foreground), the warehouse (right, foreground), and the building that housed the new Plastics Division and golf ball operations (background).

41

This building, erected in early 1962, houses the new Zippo Plastics Division and Zira Lab on Congress Street. The Zira Lab at Zippo produced the flint wheel for the lighter, and the Plastics Division produced the plastic components for Zippo flint and fuel packaging.

The new Zippo fuel plant was built adjacent to the Congress Street facility in 1966.

George G. Blaisdell's initials decorate the giant Zippo lighter being placed above the entry of the new office building at 33 Barbour Street. Construction of the three-story building began in 1954.

The new Zippo office building and adjoining factory is seen here in 1955. Zippo purchased property adjacent to the 33 Barbour Street plant and a three-story office building was constructed on the site.

George Blaisdell places his hand print in cement beneath the elaborate winding, brush-chrome staircase in the lobby of the new office building.

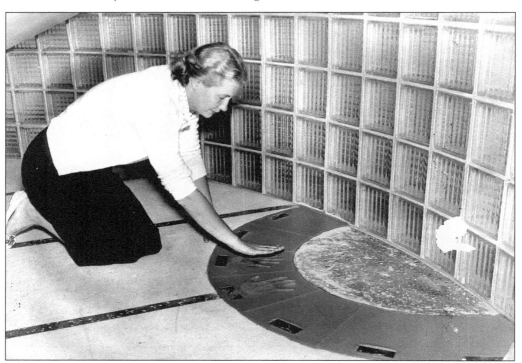

Sarah Blaisdell Dorn, one of George Blaisdell's daughters, places her hand print in the cement in the lobby of the new office building.

The Blaisdell family hand prints, imprinted in 1955, can be seen today in the lobby at Zippo. From left to right are the hand prints of grandsons George Blaisdell Duke and Paul Carnahan Duke III, daughter Sarah Blaisdell Dorn, George G. Blaisdell, daughter Harriett Blaisdell Wick, grandson David Blaisdell Wick, and granddaughter Barbara Wick Kearney.

George Blaisdell designed the Zippo lobby, reception area, and staircase of the new office building, including the ocean green and buffed terrazzo floor. The lobby was carpeted in 1973, leaving only the lighter and the Blaisdell family hand prints exposed.

George Blaisdell welcomes Bradford residents and area businessmen to the open house for the new Zippo office building in September 1955.

Bradford residents admire George Blaisdell's new office, located in the top right corner of the new building. Looking much the same today, the office is still occupied by the president and chief executive officer of Zippo Manufacturing Company.

The new office building was accessorized with custom green draperies, sporting a lighter motif. George Blaisdell ordered extra material and had two dresses made for the Zippo receptionists, Gloria Frederick (left) and Ann Stewart. Frederick kept her dress for more than 40 years and donated it to the Zippo museum in 1997. It is displayed with the original drapes.

George Blaisdell is pictured with a row of Zippo lighters lining the brick street in front of the downtown office and factory building *c.* 1955.

The Zippo Lighter Car Top was a way of promoting Zippo while out on the road in 1959. The giant lighter attached to a wooden base with large suction cups and was strapped to a car roof. The flame of the lighter was also made of wood.

One of George Blaisdell's favorite activities was to walk along Main Street in Bradford. It always took him a long time to walk just a few blocks because he stopped to chat and share a laugh with so many Bradfordians. He was known to almost everyone in this small town. These friendly greetings took place in the 1950s.

George Blaisdell engages in another "Main Street meeting" with a friend. George Blaisdell's personal appearance was always important to him, as this photograph shows, with his dapper attire and customary bow tie.

George Blaisdell walks on St. James Place toward Main Street with his nephew Howard Yates. Howard came to work at Zippo after World War II and eventually retired as vice president. In the background is the Zippo building with the famous neon sign on top. The sign is still standing today.

One of George Blaisdell's hobbies was sports cars, and he enjoyed driving his "Jag" through the hills and curves of the Allegheny Mountains that surround Bradford.

George Blaisdell devoted much time to philanthropies in his hometown. In 1952, he provided two bloodhounds to the emergency services in Bradford. Appropriately, the dogs were named Zippo and Zipette.

Introduced in 1950, the Lady Bradford offered a new elegance in the Zippo product line. Later in the 1950s, a Lady Bradford lighter graced the coffee table of the set of *I Love Lucy*. The original Lady Bradford is pictured here.

At an annual Zippo sales meeting dinner party in the 1950s, George Blaisdell took an elevated seat between his daughters, Sarah and Harriet.

This photograph of Blaisdell was used in an advertisement for Lord Calvert Whiskey. The advertisement was part of a series called "For Men of Distinction" and appeared in the March 1952 edition of *Life* magazine. The photograph was taken in his home and featured his 1933 Zippo lighter embellished with his metallique initials.

Pictured in this photograph are George Blaisdell's grandsons from his daughter, Sarah. George and Paul Duke and longtime friends Lew and Brian Zande celebrate George's birthday. Seen here are, from left to right, Brian, Lew, George, and Paul. Their friendship began as young boys because Lew and Brian's father, Lew Zande Sr., was George Blaisdell's chauffeur and right-hand man.

All three of George Blaisdell's grandsons, Paul Duke (left), Blaise Wick (middle), and George Duke, are shown here.

Here, Paul is on the left and George is on the right.

Longtime friend Lew Zande is seen here with Paul and George Duke, grandsons of George Blaisdell.

George Blaisdell sits at his desk in the new Zippo office building.

This advertisement introduced the Town and Country lighters to the Zippo product line. Most Zippo enthusiasts claim that lighters engraved by the Town and Country process are the most beautiful due to the brilliant ceramic paints that were used to create the colorful designs. The process itself was labor intensive, as each design was engraved by hand, and one color at a time was airbrushed into the cavity. The lighters were then baked to produce the vibrant colors. The last lighters to use the Town and Country process were manufactured in 1969 to commemorate the moon landing. Zippo art director and longtime employee Jack Clark was instrumental in perfecting the Town and Country process.

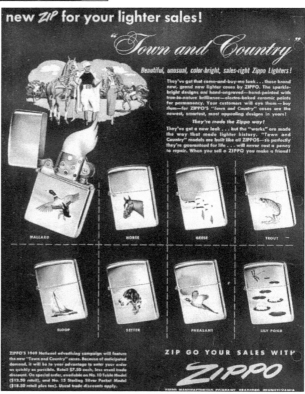

56

The first air shipment of Zippo lighters from the new Bradford Regional Airport took place in March 1951. Zippo distributor R.W. Spaulding of Meadville found that his Zippo stock was too low. Spaulding and two of his sales representatives flew to Bradford, loaded the plane with a good supply of lighters, and flew back to restock his shelves in two hours. Pictured are, from left to right, Clarence Kuntz; Bob Smith, Zippo sales executive; Joe Battaglia; and R.W. Spaulding.

Johnny, a spokesperson used in television and radio commercials for Philip Morris, with his famous, booming line "Call for Philip Morris," visits the Zippo trade show booth in the 1950s.

The Zippo plating department in the Congress Street facility ensures that the plating of Zippo lighters is consistent.

The Zippo engraving department used pantograph engraving machines to perform its work. Skilled Zippo artists engraved the design on a cardboard master. Next, the artwork was reduced in size and engraved on a brass plate. The plate was secured on the right side of the engraver and a tray of plain Zippo lighters, each beneath an engraving stylus, was secured on the left. The operator traced the design on the brass plate as it transferred on to the lighter. Once engraved, the design was painted, packaged, and shipped to the customer.

Supervisors watch as employees engrave lighters using the Gorton engraving machine in the 1960s. Pictured are, from left to right, Frances Burton, Jerome "Jerry" Miller, Gordon "Dick" Zerbe, Claude Norcross, and Betty McMurtrie. All employees shown in the photograph remained at Zippo until their retirement.

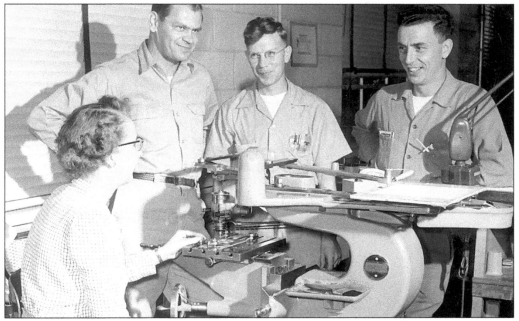

Supervisors from other departments watch as Betty Schreiber operates the Gorton engraver, making adjustments to ensure the depth and width is properly set to personalize the lighter. Pictured are, from left to right, Betty Schreiber, Mike Pehonsky, Dale Hutton, and Dick Francis. All Zippo employees shown in the photograph remained at Zippo until their retirement.

Rose Hannold operates the machine to form the chimney of the Zippo Slim lighter in the late 1970s at the Congress Street facility.

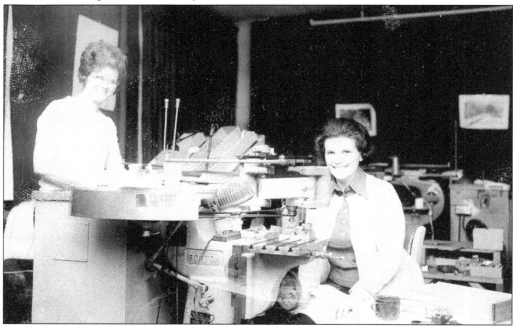

Employees Maggie Makin and Joanne Vecellio operate the signature-engraving machine at Barbour Street in the 1970s. A copy of anyone's handwritten signature could be placed on a lighter using this machine. Once engraved, the signature could be painted in a choice of colors: red, black, blue, or green.

Etching department employee Frances "Peanuts" Gorton is photographed reading a letter from President Carter in the late 1970s. Peanuts sent a note to the president saying, "I've had the name Peanuts for 49 years and I'm glad it made it to the White House." President Carter replied on official White House stationery thanking Peanuts for her special message.

The shipping department at Barbour Street celebrates Doris Greek's birthday. Pictured here are, from left to right, the following: (front) Mary Mealey, Doris Greek, Pat Lyons, Sue McCracken, Marilyn Johnson, and Mary Transue; (back) Marcia Burrell, Evelyn Carlson, Cora Wassom, two unidentified employees, Dottie Tornatella, and Harriet Speaker.

Seen in this late-1970s photograph is paint department employee Frances Johnson, who developed numerous special paints necessary to reproduce exact colors for various company logos received as commercial orders from the Ad Specialty Division of Zippo. A minimum quantity of 50 lighters is required to imprint a company logo.

Marlene McLaughlin, a paint department employee, is preparing pre-production samples for orders received from the Ad Specialty Division in this late-1970s photograph. The lighter sample is sent to the prospective company for approval. Once approved, the order is scheduled for production.

In the 1950s, 90 employees in the paint department hand painted the engraved logos on lighters.

Jerry Miller, foreman of the paint department, shares a friendly greeting with Jean Glander as she prepares imprinted Zippo product for the final step of the painting process, which is baking the imprinted lighters. This is done to ensure that the painted logo will be permanent. Both Jerry and Jean were longtime Zippo employees. This photograph was taken in 1979.

An employee attaches a Gulf emblem to a Zippo key holder using solder. The attachment of company emblems to Zippo products began in the late 1950s. These special emblem orders are part of the Ad Specialty Division. The company no longer uses solder to attach emblems.

In this late-1970s photograph, a Zippo employee checks that the lid of the lighter fits and operates properly.

Zippo employees in the Fit Up Department make adjustments to the lighters, ensuring that the inside lighting mechanism properly fits the case, in the late 1970s. Jennifer Hartle is on the right next to two unidentified people.

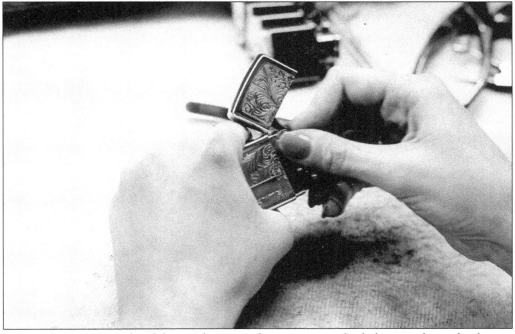

Testing for the proper fit of the inside unit is done to ensure the lighter produces the famous Zippo "click" upon opening and closing.

The television program *PM Magazine* films in the Zippo Repair Clinic in 1978. Every package containing a Zippo lighter for repair is placed in the mail bins shown in the background.

In this late-1970s photograph, repair clinic employee Grace Therminy opens a package from the mail bin. Grace was a lifelong Zippo employee and worked in the repair clinic for several years.

Laura Bacha operates the machine that stamps the Zippo logo into the bottom of the lighter case in the late 1970s. All genuine Zippo lighters carry the Zippo trademark. Today, high-speed equipment stamps the Zippo logo during the case manufacturing process.

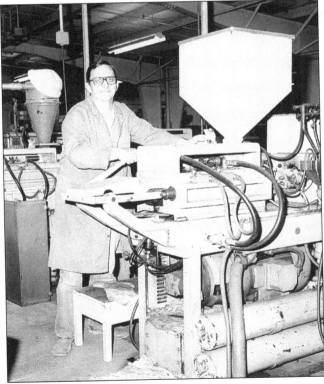

Joe Fearn of the Zippo Plastics Division examines an injection mold machine, in 1978, that makes the wheel and outer case of the flint dispenser in one operation. Joe retired from Zippo and returned as the Zippo chauffeur in the late 1990s.

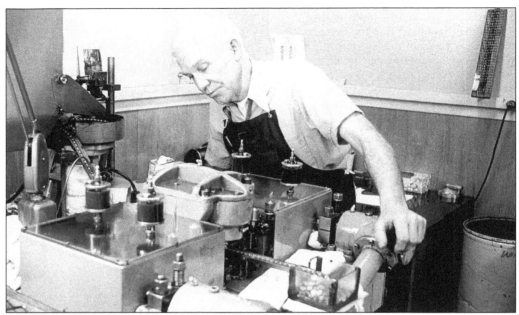

Since the 1946 wheel problem, the production of the Zippo wheel has been closely monitored for quality. Dan McGinnis checks the quality of the flint wheels as they exit the wheel-cutting machine in 1979. Dan has retired from Zippo, but his granddaughter, Theresa McGinnis Danielson, is employed in the Zippo office.

In this 1978 photograph, Mike Pehonsky, superintendent, and Brice Irons, foreman, inspect lighters that have been etched with a company logo before sending them on to the paint department. Mike retired after 47 years of service.

Dick Francis (right), assembly department foreman, shows Gary Schroeder, foreman trainee, how to replace the blade on a wick trimmer machine in 1979. Dick retired from Zippo after many years of service. Gary is the superintendent at the Congress Street facility.

John Macdonald (right), photograph screen department supervisor, shows Wayne Cawley how to make photograph screens in 1979. The screens are used to imprint company logos and designs on lighters produced for the Ad Specialty Division.

Miriam Barcroft Blaisdell, wife of George Blaisdell, passed away in 1953. Several years later, scholarships at the University of Pittsburgh at Bradford were created in her memory by the Blaisdell family.

The Blaisdell Foundation of Bradford was created in 1950 in memory of Philo and Sarah Blaisdell, George Blaisdell's parents. The Blaisdell Foundation assists the Bradford community with various needs, including this 1982 ambulance. Shown is Harriet Blaisdell Wick with Fire Chief Ted Shay in front of the Barbour Street office. Other examples of community support from Zippo and the Blaisdell Foundation include the purchase of an ambulance in 1951 and funds for construction of a new emergency room at Bradford Hospital in 1966.

In 1967, Zippo sales representatives and district managers attended the Zippo 150 Club award luncheon. The Zippo 150 Club began as a challenge to Zippo specialty sales representatives to sell 150 orders or more in one year. Pictured are, from left to right, Bob Thompson (credit manager), Al Arndt, Don Tong, Bill Mesick, Bob Sternberg, Bob Smith (in-house sales), Dave Clinton, Jim Carey, Jack Clark (Zippo art director), Bob Handloser, Don Digel (in-house sales), Bob Galey (vice president of sales), Norm Seeley, Howard Fesenmyer (in-house sales), Castex Boudreaux, Augie Leopold, Bill Feldhaus, Russ Garfield, Don Meade, Jerry Smeigh, (in-house sales), Rush St. Johns, Tom Fredericks (in-house sales), and Jack Griffith.

Zippo artist Harry Schreiber prepares art for imprinting c. 1980. Looking on is Abdul Hamid Zainal, Bahrain sales representative, and Ron Quinn, Zippo office manager.

Zippo representatives from Japanese distributor Ito Shoji visit the Barbour Street office. Photographed outside are, from left to right, Bill Jones, vice president of advertising; Mr. Miyazawa; David Seymour, Zippo Far East sales; Fumio Akasu; Howard Fesenmyer, vice president of sales; Mr. Ito; and Robert Galey, president and chief executive officer.

Zippo Japanese representatives watch as Marcia Burrell prepares the lighters to be imprinted in the etching department. From left to right are the following: (front) Mr. Miyazawa, Fumio Akasu, Mr. Ito, and Marcia Burrell; (back) Robert Smith and David Seymour.

Robert Galey, Zippo president, and Sarah Blaisdell Dorn, the owner, are seen here at the annual Zippo sales meeting, in the 1980s.

Rudy Bickel, Zippo photographer and lifelong employee, became assistant advertising manager in the 1980s. Rudy's work contributes greatly to the extensive photograph archives.

Howard Fesenmyer, vice president of sales, retired in 1991 from his lifelong work at Zippo but remains active in the company as a member of the board of directors. He is also the Blaisdell Foundation director.

Jack McCutcheon, advertising manger, and Bob Galey, president, discuss sales and marketing strategies at the 1965 Zippo sales conference.

George Blaisdell is presented with his Hole-In-One trophy at the Pennhills Country Club. The plaque on the trophy is engraved with the words "To George Blaisdell Pennhills Club October 7, 1950 6th hole 142 yards 6 Iron." Blaisdell's passion for golf was almost as strong as his passion for his lighter.

Golf balls were added to the Zippo product line in 1965. Zippo did not manufacture golf balls but imprinted them with company logos from orders received through the Ad Specialty Division. In keeping with the spirit of the game, Zippo introduced the Hole-In-One Award. Any golfer who made a hole in one using a Zippo golf ball and sent the golf ball to Zippo along with specifics of who, when, and where, was eligible to receive a gift from Zippo. The golfer had the choice of a 5.5-inch bronze trophy with the golf ball mounted and the specifics of the achievement engraved on the plaque or a brush-finished, chrome golfer lighter with the specifics engraved on the reverse. The golf ball department was located at Congress Street in the recently constructed Plastics Division building.

George Blaisdell realized another dream in 1963, when he hosted the first Zippo Open at the Pennhills Country Club in Bradford. Professional and amateur golfers from all over the United States took part in the tournament. Blaisdell is shown presenting Zippo Open winner Ted McKenzie of Philadelphia with the coveted Zippo Open trophy and prize money.

George Blaisdell and his grandchildren Blaise Wick and Barbara Wick watch the Zippo Open from under the umbrella. A little rain did not discourage golfers.

This is the clubhouse at sprawling Pennhills Country Club in Bradford. Participants in the Zippo Open always had the same comment: "one of the finest courses we ever played on."

The Zippo Men's Golf League was composed of Zippo employees. Seen here are, from left to right, the following: (front row) Tom Valentine, Bill Burgeson, and Larry Gildersleeve; (back row) Orlo Hess and Ron Quinn.

Zippo administrative secretaries keep score at the Zippo Open in 1973. They are, from left to right, Carol Feiro, Carol McDonald, and Ginny Moore. Bill Feldhaus, field manager, industrial sales, is standing.

Bob Galey (center left), president, presents the first-place trophy to Lew Zande and Carey Kaber, winners of the annual Zippo Men's Golf League outing. Howard Yates (center right), vice president, presents the second-place trophy to Tom McCord and Ed Konwinski. The tournament was followed by a barbecue for the Zippo golfers, non-golfers, and retirees at the West Branch Community Club in Bradford.

Lew Zande is pictured with George Blaisdell at the Pennhills Country Club. Lew was chauffeur and right-hand man to Blaisdell for 27 years. Lew passed away on October 3, 1976. His son Lew Zande Jr. has been employed at Zippo for 26 years.

George Blaisdell celebrates his 80th birthday in his office. Employees presented him with his special birthday cake topped with a gold Zippo lighter.

All Zippo employees were saddened at the passing of George Blaisdell on October 3, 1978. Ironically, Blaisdell passed on exactly two years to the day that his chauffeur Lew Zande Sr. passed on.

GEORGE G. BLAISDELL
1895 - 1978
FOUNDER AND PRESIDENT
ZIPPO MANUFACTURING COMPANY
THIS MEMORIAL DEDICATED TO HIS MEMORY
BY ZIPPO DISTRICT MANAGERS

| | | |
|---|---|---|
| J. WILLIAM BLACK | JAMES JOLLY | HOWARD PRYOR |
| THOMAS CAREY | CHARLES JONES | ROBERT ROCHE |
| ARTHUR DAVIDSON | DWIGHT KETCHAM, JR. | JACK SCHELLINO |
| WILLIAM DAY | LEROY KLIMA | ARTHUR SCHULTE |
| RALPH EDWARDS | ROBERT MARCHANT | EDGAR THOMAS |
| ROBERT ELLIOTT | GORDON MATHENY | RAYMOND WEINBERG |
| FRANK HIGH | | D. BLAISE WICK |

A bronze bust dedicated to the memory of George Blaisdell was given to the Blaisdell family and Zippo employees by the Zippo district managers. Jack Clark, Zippo art director, played an important role in the production of the plaque. Using a photograph, Jack molded the profile of George Blaisdell in clay, which was then cast in bronze. The plaque bears the names of the 1978 Zippo district managers.

81

With the passing of George Blaisdell, his daughters Harriet Blaisdell Wick and Sarah Blaisdell Dorn became owners of Zippo.

In commemoration of Zippo's 40th anniversary in 1972, George Blaisdell designed this lighter as a gift to all employees.

The first Zippo T-shirt was designed in 1975 and given to all employees. The Zippo sales group is shown here on Zippo T-shirt Day. From left to right are Russell Teague, Jerry Smeigh, Don Tong, Bob Galey, Bob Smith, Bill Feldhaus, and Howard Fesenmyer. The T-shirts were used in advertisements and for a consumer promotion.

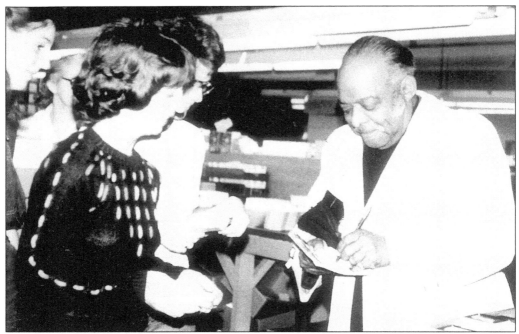

In 1978, Zippo employees receive an unexpected visit from famous musician Count Basie when he stopped to tour the Zippo plant. In this photograph, Basie signs autographs for employees Nancy Kohler and Mickey Holly of the packaging department.

Also in 1978, comedian Norm Crosby toured the Zippo plant and office, pausing to sign an autograph for secretary Ginny Jedrosko.

The Zippo office and packaging-department women challenged each other to softball games. In 1977, the Slick Chicks (packaging) beat the Zippo Zonkers (office). The next year, the Zonkers beat the Chicks. Pictured from left to right are Carol Taylor Bradish, Carol Cuthbertson Vinca, Ruthann Pascarella Kelly, and Sherry Zumstein Colella.

The annual Zippo skating party is held in March. All employees and their immediate families are invited to skate and win door prizes at the Evans Roller Drome in Bradford. Pictured in the 1980s are, from left to right, secretaries Bonnie Spry, Anne Campogiani, Bev Hull, and Betty Phillips.

Halloween is a special time at Zippo. Employees in manufacturing are permitted to wear their costumes to work as long as the costumes do not pose a risk of injury. George Blaisdell enjoyed the fun as much as his employees did. Pictured is Blaisdell with Mickey Mouse (Rosanne Pehonsky Strotman) and Minnie Mouse (Anita Davis Wolcott) in the mid-1970s.

Bette Ross, shipping foreman, is pictured here with three shipping clerks dressed in Zippo fashion as a flint dispenser, lighter, and fuel can. Bette has worked at Zippo for more years than most of her coworkers have been alive. In the summer of 2003, she celebrated 56 years of working at Zippo.

Women in the packaging department are ready to celebrate Halloween. Each Halloween, Zippo provides cider and doughnuts for employees and trick-or-treat bags for their children. Pictured from left to right are the following: (front) Karen Kemick, Marcie Drummond, Jill Chrisley, and Kathy Salerno; (back) Melanie Zandy and Debbie Prentice.

Zippo office employees participate in the bed race for the Old Home Days in 1982. From left to right are Debbie Soper, Tony Gleason, Sherry Piganelli Comilla (riding), Karen Beauseigneur, and Bonnie Spry.

Each October, the Zippo Annual Service Award dinner is held at the Pennhills Country Club in Bradford. Zippo employees are invited to celebrate their anniversary every five years. Employees with 25 years of service or more and retirees are invited to attend the annual dinner.

At the head table of this mid-1970s Annual Service Award dinner are, from left to right, Dick Francis, foreman; Frances Beers, factory employee; Tom Fredericks, personnel manager; Howard Fesenmyer, vice president; Bob Galey, president; Harriet Wick, owner; Dale Hutton, foreman; and Bob Holsinger, foreman.

A group of Zippo employees sing Christmas carols to the residents of local nursing homes sometime in the 1980s. From left to right are the following: (front) Marcia Kemick, Nancy Merry, Sandi Colosimo, Patty Thompson (Santa), Dan Zinsner, and Jean McLaughlin; (middle) Kathy Sawyer, Debbie Soper, Robin Pavone, and Keith Hoover; (back) Paul Pfaff and Fred Blackburn.

Zippo employees made the annual Christmas shopping trip to Erie in the 1980s. Zippo provides a comfortable bus and transportation for employees to enjoy a day of fun at the mall for a very reasonable cost. In front are, from left to right, Louise Case, Rose Charnisky, Claire Smeigh, Gloria Frederick, and Kay Kohler.

Everyone gathers for the annual Zippo Christmas party at the Pennhills Country Club. This gathering from the late 1970s includes, from front to back, Larry Gildersleeve, Jean McLaughlin, Carol Vinca, Sherry Piganelli, Debbie Soper, unidentified, Ed Konwinski, Jack Alviti, and Donna Vecellio.

Betty and Larry Phillips enjoy the day at Zippo's family picnic at Darien Lake in the early 1980s. Zippo invites all employees and their immediate families to be its guest at the western New York amusement park and offers a catered picnic lunch. Betty is the secretary in the marketing communications department.

A sign directs employees to the picnic pavilions at Darien Lake.

Employees enjoy their ride on the *Viper* roller coaster at Darien Lake at the picnic.

Homemade*

Homemade Pie by Marlene Lee, Zippo Employee

Every ZIPPO lighter is made with loving care right here in America, with a tradition of American craftsmanship. And it's guaranteed to work always, or we'll fix it free. Any way you slice it, it's as American as apple pie.

*In Bradford, Pa. U.S.A.

ZIPPO

This advertisement ran in the June 1983 edition of *Reader's Digest*, signifying that the Zippo lighter is as homemade as apple pie. The advertisement features the award-winning pie made by employee Marlene Frantz.

Early in 1983, Bill Jones, vice president of advertising, announced that an employee contest would take place for baking apple pies. There would be a cash prize and the best-looking pie would be photographed and used in the "homemade as apple pie" advertisement. Marlene Frantz was the winner. The remaining pies were sliced and eaten by employees. From left to right are Doris Greek, Mary ?, Helen Kightlinger, Dee Timblin, and Angie Armagost.

In commemoration of Zippo's 50th anniversary in 1982, employees and their families were invited to tour the Zippo facilities and see the replication of the original Zippo factory on display. The sign on the easel left of the window says "Thank you Bradford, It's been a great 50 years," and it contains the signatures of all Zippo employees.

The 200-millionth Zippo lighter rolls off the production line on September 23, 1988. Zippo owner Sarah Dorn and president Michael Schuler watch as Harriet Wick, owner, places the packaged lighter into the box.

93

The Zippo advertising theme for 1980 was a takeoff of the presidential election of that year. Lighters were produced with the donkey and elephant logos representing the political parties. Red, white, and blue hats and campaign buttons were distributed and worn at the annual sales meeting and trade shows. Zippo artist Rita Walters sports the hat and button beside the Select Zippo campaign banner.

*Five*

# Into the 21st Century

Attracting thousands of visitors from more than 120 countries since its opening in 1997, the Zippo/Case Visitors Center has become northern Pennsylvania's most visited museum. The visitors center features a world-class museum, the Zippo Repair Clinic and the Zippo/Case Store. Outside are 14 lighter-shaped street lighters that are illuminated with windproof flames, and, when not on the road traveling, the re-created famous Zippo car is on display.

In 1992, the Barbour Street office building received a facelift. Due to safety concerns, the distinct, black carrera glass panels placed on the office building in 1955 were removed. The new replacement outer shell consisted of a granite base and dark-green glass panels, made of modern tempered glass, mounted on a metal grid attached separately to the building.

At the Congress Street manufacturing facility, construction began in 1992 to add a large warehouse addition, a second floor to accommodate more office space, and enclose all buildings except the Zippo fuel plant. In record time, the additions and construction were completed, and the goal was achieved.

Zippo Manufacturing Company celebrated its 60th anniversary in 1992 in coordination with its international sales meeting. Balloons were shaped into the number 60 and placed on the gazebo at the University of Pittsburgh at Bradford, where the sales meeting events were held.

Zippo representatives from around the world attended the sales meeting and celebration commemorating the 60th anniversary. In the front row, from left to right, are sales managers Bill Galey, Mike Martin, and Chris Keller.

Zippo employees and their spouses were invited for a fun-filled day to celebrate Zippo's 60th anniversary at the University of Pittsburgh at Bradford.

Employees play volleyball at the anniversary celebration.

W.R. Case & Sons Cutlery became a Zippo subsidiary in May 1993. Case is one of the most respected names in the cutlery industry, making a natural union of the two companies best known for a quality product. Holgate, which made high-quality wooden toys, was an affiliated company in the early 1990s.

The first Zippo Family Store and Museum opened in late 1993 under the guidance of Pat Grandy, Rudy Bickel, Peggy Errera, and Mike McLaughlin. The building adjacent to the manufacturing facility on Congress Street was purchased from the Race automobile dealership. This Zippo building now houses the Zippo Promotional Products Division.

Here is a section of the museum at the original Zippo Family Store and Museum.

Zippo employees and ABC radio personalities Jim Zippo and Maria Danza stand outside the Zippo Family Store and Museum in celebration of the first National Zippo Day, held in 1994. The film crew of the A.M. *Buffalo* morning show from Buffalo, New York, came to Bradford and aired this clip on their show.

Pat Grandy and Peggy Errera are pictured with radio celebrities Jim Zippo and Maria Danza. With a name such as Jim Zippo, Zippo naturally wanted him to broadcast from the first National Zippo Day and Zippo/Case International Swap Meet events.

The 300-millionth lighter was produced on April 15, 1996. To commemorate this significant event, a celebration took place in the Zippo factory.

Zippo owners Harriett Blaisdell Wick and Sarah Blaisdell Dorn hold the 300 millionth lighter, in 1996, with their sons in the background. Their sons are, from left to right, George Duke, Blaise Wick, and Paul Duke.

Zippo factory employees were invited to partake in the 300-millionth-lighter celebration.

Bette Ross and Wayne Bartlett, employees with the most years of service, were invited to participate in the celebration. Bette had been employed at Zippo for 46 years and Wayne for 45 years.

The Zippo/Case Visitors Center, located at 1932 Zippo Drive, features the Zippo/Case Store, museum, and Zippo Repair Clinic. The former Zippo Family Store and Museum could not accommodate the large number of visitors, so plans for a new facility three times larger were created in 1996. The visitors center opened in July 1997, and Pennsylvania governor Tom Ridge toured the facility on the second day it was open. Pat Grandy, marketing communications manager, led the team that created the museum's archival and interactive displays. Two of the most popular attractions in the museum are ZAC (Zippo and Case), an audio-kinetic ball machine, and the up-close view of the Zippo Repair Clinic. The museum exhibits were designed by Steve Feldman Design.

Zippo celebrated its 65th anniversary in 1997, in conjunction with the international sales meeting and the Zippo/Case International Swap Meet. The formal dedication of the new Zippo/ Case Visitors Center took place at the same time. Sarah Dorn is shown speaking at the official dedication with family members and executives looking on. Paul Duke is seen to the left of the podium. To the right of the podium are, from left to right, a former employee, George Brinkley, Pat Grandy, Barbara Wick Kearney, Blaise Wick, and George Duke.

The entrance of the Zippo/Case Visitors Center greets visitors with a giant moving sculpture of Zippo high-polish chrome lighters and Case pearl-handled knives rotating around a world globe. The 7-by-11-foot American flag composed of 3,393 red, white, and blue Zippo lighters is located to the left of the sculpture.

Shown is the seven-foot, audio-kinetic ball machine located in the museum. Zippo commissioned George Rhoads of Ithaca, New York, to design an attraction for young people visiting the museum. Both children and adults are mesmerized by the motions, sounds, and colors produced by its gears, chimes, chutes, and climbs. The new ball machine needed a name, and keeping with the traditional Zippo spirit, a contest was developed for all Zippo employees to select a suitable name. Employee Kelly Rose Platko won the contest with the name ZAC, which stands for "Zippo and Case."

Mike Martin, Zippo vice president of sales, welcomes friends and collectors from all over the world to the 2000 Zippo/Case International Swap Meet. Zippo and Case have hosted six international swap meets. The next meet is scheduled for July 2004.

Zippo and Case guests enjoy the traditional outdoor barbeque held in conjunction with the Zippo/Case International Swap Meet.

Zippo owner George Duke visits with international Zippo distributors at the Zippo/Case International Swap Meet. From left to right are Joe Romei (Italy), George Duke, Rolf Loeser (Germany), Guido Heuvelmann (Germany), and Antonio Gagean (Portugal).

Linda Meabon explains Zippo history to a lighter collector at the 1995 Zippo/Case International Swap Meet.

Zippo lighter and Case knife collectors display their coveted collections beneath the giant tents at the swap meet that is held on the grounds of the Zippo/Case Visitors Center. Collections are beautifully displayed on 200 tables at the swap meet, in addition to the giant sale tent of Zippo and Case merchandise and other special events. Zippo lighter and Case knife collectors that were members of the collector clubs On the Lighter Side, Pocket Lighter Preservation Guild, and the Case Collectors Club were invited to display their lighters and knives at the swap meet. To commemorate each swap meet, a special, imprinted Zippo lighter, Case knife, and Zippo-lighter-and-Case-knife set are produced in limited numbers for purchase at the event.

A couple of avid Zippo collectors discuss their latest acquisitions at the swap meet. Tom Prylinski is on the left, and Karen Politi is on the right.

Winston, the Zippo/Case International Swap Meet mascot, visited the swap meet every year with his parents, Woodie and Gary Sneary. Winston was suitably outfitted for the 1997 meet.

Avid Zippo collectors Beverley and Wally Laird take time to browse through the swap meet tents, looking for the Zippo lighter not yet in their collection. Wally was the first Zippo collector that contacted Linda Meabon at Zippo, in the mid-1980s, inquiring about particular lighters and requesting the history of the imprinted company logo.

Sherry Piganelli Comilla, Zippo switchboard operator, speaks her famous greeting "Good morning, Zippo-o-o-o" on the radio at the 1997 Zippo/Case International Swap Meet. Sherry was known to Zippo customers all over the world as the "voice of Zippo." From left to right are Maria Danza, Sherry, and Jim Zippo.

Another popular Zippo/Case International Swap Meet event is the Motorcycle Dice Run. The local group of motorcycle riders gather for an organized ride through the Allegheny National Forest, under the direction of Dave Geitner of Bradford. The entry fee charged for the ride is donated to the Kids with Cancer program through the Bradford Hospital Foundation.

Participants of the Motorcycle Dice Run line up in front of the Zippo/Case Visitors Center. The line runs all the way past the manufacturing facility. Their ride commences at the visitors center and continues down Main Street in Bradford.

The 50th-anniversary celebration of Zippo Canada was held at the Zippo/Case Visitors Center in 1999. All employees of the Zippo Canada facility came to Bradford for the event. Two Canadian flags were made of red and white Zippo lighters. One of the flags was presented to the employees of Zippo Canada, and the other is displayed in the Zippo/Case Visitors Center. Zippo Canada had manufacturing operations from 1949 to 2002.

Zippo and Case employees enjoy the 2001 employee picnic held in August of every year on the grounds of the Zippo/Case Visitors Center. The company owners provide good food, games, and music for all employees in appreciation of their hard work. Seated from left to right are Chris Lechner, Carol Bradish, Martha Keefe, Donna Whitford, and Dorie Meabon.

The Zippo and Case employee picnic provides a time for employees and retirees of both Zippo and Case to relax and enjoy a day of fun. Julio Pedine (center) retired from Zippo's art department after 42 years of service.

Zippo became involved in motorsports in the 1990s and sponsored NASCAR Bush Series driver Jimmy Spencer. Zippo currently sponsors TF Racing, which includes drivers such as John Kohler, Gary Smith, Michael DeFontes, David Brown, and Todd Houk. The team competes in the Grand-Am Cup Street Stock Series. Zippo also sponsors the Zippo U.S. Vintage Grand Prix of Watkins Glen, New York. From left to right are Mike Schuler, Jimmy Spencer, and George Duke.

Show here is one of the TF Racing Cobra R Mustang cars on the track at Watkins Glen, New York.

Zippo owner George Duke takes Zippo employee Bonnie Spry for a spin around the track in his Porsche before the start of the Zippo U.S. Vintage Grand Prix.

George Duke presents a trophy to the winner of the 1998 Zippo U.S. Vintage Grand Prix. Zippo has sponsored this race since 1991.

Greg Booth, president and chief executive officer of Zippo Manufacturing Company, joined the company in 2001. Previously, he was the president and chief operating officer for W.R. Case & Sons Cutlery, a wholly owned subsidiary of Zippo. Booth is a native of Bradford.

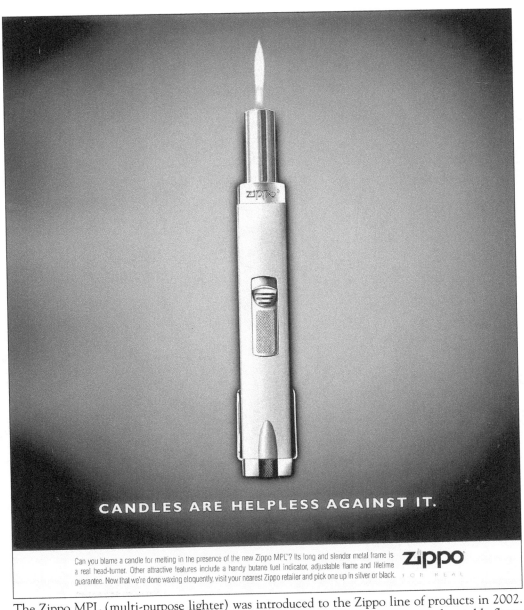

**CANDLES ARE HELPLESS AGAINST IT.**

Can you blame a candle for melting in the presence of the new Zippo MPL? Its long and slender metal frame is a real head-turner. Other attractive features include a handy butane fuel indicator, adjustable flame and lifetime guarantee. Now that we're done waxing eloquently, visit your nearest Zippo retailer and pick one up in silver or black.

**zippo**
FOR REAL

The Zippo MPL (multi-purpose lighter) was introduced to the Zippo line of products in 2002. The butane lighter is refillable and can be used in numerous ways as a source of portable flame for campfires, grills, and candles.

In the 1990s, the company introduced the concept of employee participation by forming groups to implement strategic plans. The members of this group implemented the idea of a corporate-based, Zippo-lighter collectors club, known as Zippo Click, because of the increasing number of Zippo lighter collectors. Seen here are, from left to right, the following: (front) Peggy Errera, Violet Snyder, and Shirley Evers; (back) Jeff Bosworth, Jerry Johnson Jr., Linda Meabon, and Star Davis.

Kathleen Jones is the Zippo Click collector's club administrator. The official kick-off of Zippo Click was July 2002, and one year later, it has more than 2,600 members from around the world.

The first Zippo Click collector's club lighter was a 1941-replica Zippo lighter imprinted with the Zippo Click logo. The lighter was packaged in a special click-clack tin featuring a montage of Zippo memorabilia from the archives.

Zippo continues its role as a pop-culture icon sparked by a community of Zippo tricksters on Zippotricks.com. Web site founder Morton Kjolberg, of Norway, regards Zippo tricks as part sport and part performance art. Whatever the reason, performing tricks using the Zippo lighter has definitely caught on with young adults around the world. Seen here are, from left to right, trickster Richard Kimzey (also known as Mr. Twistyneck), Morton Kjolberg, and trickster Erik Elliott (also known as Booty).

Booty and Mr. Twistyneck get tricky with their Zippo lighters. They have appeared at numerous public performances and on both local and national television.

Shown is an original 1933 Zippo lighter with a metallique golfer. This unique lighter was purchased by Zippo from Madeline Miles during the 2002 Zippo/Case International Swap Meet and is now on display at the Zippo/Case Visitors Center.

Madeline Miles and Jim Guelfi, a friend of Madeline's, hold the original 1933 metallique golfer lighter. Madeline found the lighter, which belonged to her grandfather, "Bill" Hansel William Loveland, who at the time of his retirement was chairman and president of the board of Bradford National Bank. Loveland was an advocate for promoting the community of Bradford. Madeline continued to support the community, as her grandfather did, by donating the proceeds of the lighter to various Bradford agencies.

George Duke poses with the Zippo car in Las Vegas in early 2003. The new Zippo car, or "Zippo II," as it reads on the license plate, is a 1997 re-creation of the original Zippo car (page 29). Like the original, it was fabricated from a 1947 Chrysler Saratoga.

George Blaisdell sits at his desk in the Barbour Street office lighting the Austrian-designed lighter. The Blaisdell family signet ring is shown on his left pinkie finger. Only seven signet rings were commissioned and all belong to Blaisdell's descendants. The imprinted ring design is a cast in a mirror or reverse image. The design shows a lighter, the phrase "1933 Bradford Penna," and the word "Laborant," which means "they work." The ring is reminiscent of those worn in the 1700s that were used to secure the family crest in hot wax on a document or envelope.

As part of Zippo's 70th anniversary commemoration in 2002, owners Sarah Dorn and George Duke commissioned 300 solid-gold, 1941 replica lighters as a tribute to founder George G. Blaisdell. Each lighter was engraved with the same reverse image of the family signet ring. The lighter was engraved using a pantograph machine. This is a method that has not been used by Zippo since the early 1970s. A solid granite plaque adorned the lid of the cherry presentation box. The lid also displays a laser-engraved image of the signet design. A special bottom stamp authenticates the lighter as the G.G.B 1941 model. A certificate of authenticity is hand numbered to match the lighter inside and was personally signed by Sarah Dorn and George Duke.

Grant Barcroft Duke (left) and George Blaisdell Duke Jr. (right) are the sons of Zippo owner George Duke and the grandsons of Zippo owner Sarah Dorn.

Posed in front of a portrait of George Blaisdell are George Duke and his mother, Sarah Dorn, who follow Blaisdell's philosophies by producing high-quality products, supporting the community of Bradford, and treating their employees like family.

Lightning Source UK Ltd.
Milton Keynes UK
UKHW031906270622
405049UK00004B/144

9 781531 608446